CW01642110

A NEW HOLY WEEK GUIDE FOR SERVERS AND SACRISTANS

A New Holy Week Guide for SERVERS & SACRISTANS

Edward Matthews

McCrimmons
Great Wakering, Essex, United Kingdom

First published in United Kingdom in 2006 by
McCRIMMON PUBLISHING CO. LTD.,
1012 High Street, Great Wakering,
Essex, SS3 0EQ, England
www.mccrimmons.com
info@mccrimmons.com

ISBN 0 85597 668 3

Nihil obstat	Mgr. G.B. Stokes *Censor Deputatus*
Imprimatur	+ Thomas McMahon *Bishop of Brenwood*

Cover illustration: The Benedictine Sisters of Turvey Abbey
Cover design: Nick Snode
Printed by Thanet Press Ltd., Margate, Kent

Contents

Good Friday

The Easter Vigil

Author's note

This guide first saw the light of day in 1972. Since then much has happened to make that version out of date: a definitive version of the Roman Missal/ Sacramentary was published in 1974 (an interim version had been in use at the time), and the Rite of Christian Initiation of Adults (RCIA) appeared in 1987. The promulgation of the English language version of the RCIA made a huge difference to the liturgy of the Easter Vigil and to our understanding of Christian Initiation in general. This required extensive revision of the chapter on the Easter Vigil.

The original guide also betrayed the age and context in which it was originally written. Parish communities today are liturgically more knowledgeable and experienced than they were over thirty years ago, so much so I had doubts about going ahead with this revision, but I was persuaded there was a need.

In an earlier revision an appendix included the description of the Easter Vigil celebrated in an order different from that in the Roman Missal/Sacramentary (the blessing of the fire etc. taking place at the conclusion of the Old Testament readings). I am now satisfied that was liturgically unsound and so have omitted it from the present guide.

Introduction

THE EASTER TRIDUUM, beginning with the Mass of the Lord's Supper on Holy Thursday, continuing through the celebration of the Lord's Passion on Good Friday and culminating in the Easter Vigil, is the heart of the Church's entire year. 'What Sunday is to the week, the solemnity of Easter is to the liturgical year', say the official norms for the liturgical year.[1] We can celebrate nothing greater.

Palm Sunday (or Passion Sunday, as it is also known) is the gateway to that supreme celebration. It is appropriate and practical, therefore, to include in one Guide all the major parish celebrations of Holy Week, the Great Week.

The Church's liturgy is the celebration, the worship of the entire community[2]: all ministers, priests, musicians, servers, sacristans and so forth, serve each other so that the celebration may truly be worship by the whole community. Altar servers, though many of

1 General Norms for the Liturgical Year and the Calendar, Rome 1969.

2 Constitution on the Sacred Liturgy, Vatican II, no. 7.

their tasks centre upon the priest, are assisting the wider community to pray, to worship. This truth must be the bedrock of their training. The practical side of serving obviously engages the attention of servers and their leaders (and that is what this booklet is about) but it is not end in itself. The true end is a prayerful and dynamic encounter between God and the Church.

This encounter takes place in a human way – through words, music, light, colour, movement, gesture, silence. All that is human has a place in the liturgy. The 'marriage' of the material and the spiritual, the human and divine in our liturgy, is a real continuation of the Incarnation when Jesus, Son of God, took on our human nature so that we might become sharers in the divine nature.

Servers, by their skills, their dignity, their prayerfulness, contribute to an overall sense of mystery which should imbue all good liturgy. They do not call attention to themselves, and yet if they were altogether missing, the celebration would be very much the poorer. Ceremonial is itself the servant of the liturgy and of the community: consequently the servers who carry it out bear a great responsibility.

In their turn, servers' leaders, masters of ceremonies, should be particularly aware of their 'servant' role in the preparation and carrying out of the liturgy, of which they will have a deep love and knowledge. For Holy Week, the starting points are the

Roman Missal/Sacramentary[3], the Lectionary and the RCIA: a thorough acquaintance with these is an essential foundation. With this under their belt, MCs are able not only to guide the servers immediately under their direction but also coordinate with presiding priest, musicians, ministers, and others with tasks in the celebration. A master of ceremonies is not a dictator but one who integrates the ministry of the servers with the worship of the wider community.

Servers give of their best when they know what they are celebrating and have an overall view of the structure of the celebration: their preparation for Holy Week is best begun when the leader first 'tells the story' of the rites and walks them through the action. This booklet aims to help that process with a brief introduction to the meaning of each celebration and some general ideas about how it is to be carried out, followed by a more detailed guide to the rite.

Because liturgical worship is public prayer it is good that servers begin their practices and actual celebrations with a shared prayer, perhaps one adapted from the liturgy about to be celebrated: that prayer then continues into the celebration. Some

3 The officially approved English translation of the Missale Romanum for England, Wales, Scotland, Ireland and Australia is entitled Roman Missal, the USA edition is entitled Sacramentary, and is used in a number of communities outside USA. Therefore we refer to Roman Missal/Sacramentary throughout.

ministers (servers, musicians) feel that they have not prayed while performing their ministerial duties, and that is understandable from a particular, but narrow, point of view. Everything that contributes to the liturgy is prayer. The ceremonial, ritual gestures, the worry and the distractedness of ministers with special responsibilities, and so much more besides, are all part of its pattern. It is not words alone that constitute prayer, but also actions, gestures, movement, music, and silence.

Servers should carry out their duties with a calm dignity: this contributes to the prayerful spirit of the community. Conversely, frenetic activity, fussiness, or an overly casual approach to serving affects others present at the celebration and threatens their wholehearted participation. Experience teaches that masters of ceremonies are sometimes particular offenders in this matter. Things go wrong, but their correction by overwrought reaction frequently compounds the mistake: now everybody knows there has been a slip-up. If possible, it is better to let a mistake run its natural course when the server may realise the error and put it right: meanwhile the community, if it has noticed at all, will assume it is simply another element of the relatively unfamiliar Holy Week liturgy

Good liturgy requires a sense of humour, in the sense that we should not take ourselves too seriously, whether we are serving, singing, presiding, reading, or carrying out any of the other myriad ministries. Deep in our hearts we detect the joy, gifted by the Holy Spirit, in being part of Christ's worship of the Father. With all our faults and all our gifts we are caught up in the work of our salvation, the Paschal Mystery. What a work, what a joy!

* * *

IN GENERAL

THE NUMBER OF SERVERS

The lists of servers in this booklet indicate the number required for celebrations in a medium-sized church. There can be no hard and fast rule because each community is different. Recent years have witnessed a rise in the number of regular servers in many parishes, partly, if not largely, due to the lifting of the official ban on girls.

As far as possible, tasks should be shared out among all the servers: avoid disappointing regular year-round servers who sometimes find themselves side-lined on more solemn occasions in favour of less regular but older servers. Parishes with slimmer resources should be able to double up on certain tasks after having considered whether all of them are really necessary.

The term 'Acolyte' is used here to denote candle-bearer. While this is not technically correct, it has a popular understanding and is used here in that sense.

Other Ministries

Lay readers are presumed to be a regular part of any celebration and so are not normally mentioned in the lists later in this booklet. The reader, carrying the Lectionary with dignity, may be included in a liturgy's entry procession, or he/she may approach the place for the Reading immediately before it takes place, or they may already be in place, close to the ambo.

Lay Eucharistic ministers perform their duties in ways different from parish to parish, and nothing can be firmly laid down except to recommend dignity and reverence. In Holy Week there will often be a need for more than the usual number of ministers: the ministers' coordinator or the master of ceremonies should prepare for this.

Gospel Processions

Throughout the liturgical year the proclamation of the Gospel is usually accompanied by servers carrying lighted candles and thurible. (Just as we light candles and use incense to show honour to Christ present in the Sacrament, so we show honour to the Living Word present in the proclamation.)

Holy Week is different. The Roman Missal/Sacramentary explicitly excludes these ministries at the reading of the Passion on Palm Sunday and Good Friday, and only incense is carried at the gospel of the Easter Vigil (although many parish communities do not take note of this). Lights and incense are carried at the reading of the Procession gospel on Palm Sunday and at the gospel of Holy Thursday's Evening Mass of the Lord's Supper.

Procession at the Preparation of the Gifts

The bearing of the gifts of bread and wine for the Eucharist by members of the congregation should be standard practice, at least on Sundays and at other major celebrations.

Should servers (maybe with lighted candles) lead this procession? The present writer once favoured this practice, but now it seems to him to clericalise an action which should be specifically lay oriented. If candles are deemed useful to highlight the solemnity of this rite, they might be carried by lay members of the congregation and placed on or near the altar at the conclusion of the procession.

Palm Sunday

INTRODUCTION

TODAY'S CELEBRATION is divided into two distinct parts: the Commemoration of the Lord's Entrance into Jerusalem, and the Mass. The best start to your preparation for the Lord's Entrance is to read the designated Gospel account for the current year of the Lectionary cycle, noting that in Year B St John's Gospel can be used as an alternative. Then, reading through the prayers and chants, notice how the emphasis is upon Christ as triumphant King, rather than victim for sacrifice. The procession has the character of a royal progress, of the entry of a king into his kingdom. This can be enhanced by the informal waving of the palms by the congregation, conveying a sense of joy and welcome. An obstacle to this idea is the common practice of plaiting the palms in the form of a cross – a practice that seems not to be quite in tune with this part of the celebration. But we do not ignore the suffering that is to come: the procession with palms gives us a foretaste of the glory which will come through Christ's Passion. So, in the words of the presiding priest's suggested introduction, "Christ entered in triumph into his own city, to complete his work as our Messiah: to suffer, to die, and to rise again." (cf. Roman Missal/Sacramentary).

Like all liturgy, participation is the key to a successful celebration, and this means the participation of the entire community. In planning the liturgy consideration must be given to involving everybody in the procession: it is their entrance to the celebration of Holy Week and the Easter Triduum. An involving and meaningful liturgy will be an aperitif for the rest of the week, especially for those who have had little or no experience of its celebrations in the past.

Make sure everyone is provided with sufficient palms or some other greenery; it is all too easy to focus on the servers to the exclusion of others. Make sure everyone can see the presiding priest; help the entire community to be true participants and not just incidental spectators. The ritual gestures and movements of the servers will be dignified and simple, enhancing the celebration and not overloading it with unnecessary flourishes. The spirit of the servers' movements and gestures should be the natural outcome of all that the entire worshipping community is doing together, rather than something separate and special; servers minister to the community's worship.

The Liturgy

1. The Roman Missal/Sacramentary provides three ways of commemorating the Lord's entrance into Jerusalem: the Procession; the Solemn Entrance; the Simple Entrance. This is based on the premise of a parish community which regularly designates one of its Masses as the principal Mass of the day, and during which it makes the greatest use of its musical and other ministerial resources. While that may be true of many communities, there are others which celebrate the Sunday liturgy in a variety of ways (e.g. adapted celebrations for children) so that what is 'principal' for one section of the community may not be so for another. Each parish community will therefore plan its own celebration accordingly.

2. Since we are celebrating the entrance of the Lord into Jerusalem the rite should take place outside the sanctuary (for exactly where, see below): the meaning of the procession is somewhat nullified if it begins and ends there. The Roman Missal/Sacramentary also indicates that the palm branches (and whatever other greenery is used) are to be distributed before the celebration begins. On the other hand, The Ceremonial of Bishops (published in 1984) envisages the bishop distributing palms to the clergy, but this should

be seen as an exception. In any case, the physical circumstances of many churches makes ritual distribution difficult or even chaotic.

3. First Form: The Procession

Choose a place separate from the church for the Blessing of Palms and beginning of the procession. It should be large enough to accommodate the community and enable them easily to participate. A school or parish hall, garden, playground are some of the possible venues: immediately outside the church entrance is not recommended, though some city parishes may be hard pressed to find anywhere better. Make sure provision is made (by welcomers or notices) to direct people to the place where the celebration is to begin.

4. Presiding priest and servers should assemble close to the starting point, thus ensuring that those responsible for preparing the place do not have to make long journeys to and from the church.

5. Form servers and celebrant:

❊ *Thurifer*

❊ *Acolyte 1 – Cross – Acolyte 2*

❊ *Holy Water and Book-bearers*

❊ *Other servers*

❊ *Book of the Gospels (deacon or server)*

❊ *Celebrant*

6. Go to the place of Blessing and stand there in such a way that the cross-bearer, flanked by Acolytes, do not obscure the view of the community. The book-bearer is to the left of the celebrant: the holy water-bearer to his right. The thurifer stands well to one side. Because the book is to be carried from place to place, it is safer to put it in the constant charge of a server from the outset; its eventual arrival back at the church is thus more likely.

7. The celebrant makes the sign of the cross and greets the people as at Mass (book-bearer). He introduces the celebration, reads the prayer of blessing, and sprinkles the branches (holy water-bearer). To do this he may or may not walk among the people: the layout of the location dictates what course to take.

8. The gospel account of the Lord's entrance is proclaimed by a deacon, a priest, or, lacking those, the celebrant. Incense and candles are carried as at a solemn Mass. Use either a portable lectern or a server to support the Book of the Gospels. The celebrant may deliver a brief homily.

9. Incense is put in the thurible and the procession forms as in 5, on p.20. The celebrant carries a palm. The people follow immediately after the celebrant. Make sure the procession is not too fast, particularly as it begins, because it can take some time for people to gather together in processional form.

10. Process to the church and into the sanctuary. Servers go to their usual Mass places.
The celebrant may cense the altar, if he wishes. If he is wearing a cope, he changes to a chasuble. He concludes the procession by reading the Opening Prayer of the Mass. The Liturgy of the Word follows in the usual way.

11. Second Form: The Solemn Entrance

This is for churches where there is no convenient and separate place to celebrate the blessing, and no possibility of a procession outside the church. Instead the blessing and the other rites of the First Form take place at or near the entrance to the church. The Roman Missal/Sacramentary suggests representatives of the community may take part in the procession; the feasibility of this will depend on local circumstances.

12. **Third Form: The Simple Entrance**

According to the Roman Missal/Sacramentary this rite takes place if there is no solemn entrance (see: 11, on p.21), and it is no more than the normal entry of priest and ministers. However many parish communities celebrate the Second Form at all Masses as a matter of course, apart from the Mass at which the First Form is celebrated, and there is no reason why this should not be so.

13. The account of the Passion is read, if possible, by a group taking different parts as indicated in the Lectionary. The part of Christ is traditionally reserved to the celebrant, but this is not an absolute rule. There are no greeting or signs of the cross at the beginning. Candles and incense are not carried.

Palm Sunday check list

SERVERS

- ❍ Cross-bearer
- ❍ Acolyte 1
- ❍ Acolyte 2
- ❍ Thurifer
- ❍ Book-bearer
- ❍ Holy water-bearer

SACRISTY (or, convenient room cf. no.4, on p.19)

- ❍ Alb
- ❍ Chasuble or cope (red)
- ❍ Thurible, lighted
- ❍ Incense
- ❍ Processional cross, unveiled and decorated with palms
- ❍ 2 Acolyte's candles
- ❍ Holy water
- ❍ Roman Missal / Sacramentary
- ❍ Lectionary/Book of the Gospel
- ❍ Gospel decorated with palms
- ❍ Palms for celebrant and servers
- ❍ Palms for people at a place where they can be conveniently picked up (there is no distribution during the celebration)

SANCTUARY

- ❍ All as usual for Mass (red chasuble, if cope is used for blessing and procession)
- ❍ Extra Lectionaries / Book of the Gospel for Passion
- ❍ Microphones and book stands as necessary

Holy Thursday

INTRODUCTION

THE EVENING MASS of the Lord's Supper is the beginning of the Easter Triduum. 'Triduum' means 'three days' and is a reference to the three days culminating in the celebration of the Lord's resurrection. The three liturgies of these days – Evening Mass of the Lord's Supper, the Lord's Passion, and the Easter Vigil – are in reality a single celebration, the Lord's Passover. We are on a journey with him from the upper room, through his passion, and so to his resurrection.

Helping servers to understand this enables them to gain greater benefit from this, the greatest of all the Church's liturgies, and encourages them to attend all three days.

A prayerful reading of the day's gospel is essential before any liturgical planning, followed by a thorough reading of the rite as set out in the Roman Missal/Sacramentary. The main structure is that of Mass, with the incorporation of the Washing of the Feet after the homily and the Transfer of the Holy Eucharist at the end.

The mood of the celebration undergoes a distinct change at the 'Glory to God in the highest' during which the church bells may be rung and then remain silent until the Easter Vigil. The organ and other musical instruments are played only to support the singing: no interludes or the like. It is as if the Church first rejoices in God's great gift to us of the Eucharist, and then sombrely reflects on the cost of this sacrifice.

The Washing of the Feet has taken a long time to be accepted in parishes but is now a treasured part of the liturgy in many places. The number of people to have their feet washed is not laid down in the Roman Missal/Sacramentary, though most communities favour twelve, corresponding to the number of apostles. The Roman Missal/Sacramentary is not so reticent about the gender of the participants: men are the only ones mentioned. Some say that this restriction arises from the all-male apostles present at the Last Supper. But our liturgy is not a 'video replay' of past events: rather, it is a celebration of the truth that, like our Master, we must serve each other, including women. Others argue against the washing of women's feet on the grounds of delicacy: a little common sense should eliminate any foreseen problems.

The location of the Washing of Feet depends largely upon the design and physical layout of the church. On the one hand, we should avoid subjecting the participants to unnecessary stress; on the other, it is important that the rest of the community should see what is going on. Locating each participant at the end of a pew, or row of seats, underlines the sense of service to the whole community: visibility, however, could then be a problem. (In all liturgical celebrations we should remember that the ministers' grandstand view of proceedings may not be shared by the rest of the community: in planning liturgy, always ask the question, 'What will the people see?') The sanctuary is probably the most popular choice of location.

An unofficial but welcome addition to the liturgy found in some places is the presentation of the newly blessed oils before the Penitential Rite: the oil of baptism/catechumens perhaps presented by the parents of a baby soon to be baptised, the oil of the sick by a sick person or nurse or doctor, the oil of chrism by one preparing for confirmation. These are simply suggestions. The presentation of the oils underlines the unity between diocese and parish and reminds the local community of the sacraments which give it life.

The Liturgy

1. Form the entry procession in the usual way:

    ⁜ *Thurifer*

    ⁜ *Acolyte 1 – Cross – Acolyte 2*

    [Readers and Ministers of Communion]

    ⁜ *Other servers*

    ⁜ *Deacon bearing Book of the Gospels*

    ⁜ *Concelebrants*

    ⁜ *Presiding celebrant*

2. Incense is put in the thurible and the thurifer leads the procession to the sanctuary where the presiding priest puts in more incense, if necessary, and censes the altar. He takes his place at the chair, greets the people and receives the blessed oils (see Introduction, above); these should then be placed on a table, perhaps with a lighted candle. (The altar is to be used only as a last resort because of confusion with the Eucharistic gifts.) The priest then leads the Penitential Rite, intones the 'Glory be to God in the highest' and bells are rung (see Introduction, above).

The Readings are proclaimed as usual, the Gospel being accompanied by incense and Acolytes bearing candles; a homily is delivered.

3. The Washing of Feet

The presiding celebrant is helped by Acolyte 1 to remove his chasuble (optional but practical); Acolyte 2 helps him to put on an apron (usually an amice tied around the waist). While bearing in mind our earlier warning to avoid making the liturgy appear to be a 'video replay' of Jesus' actions, these simple actions help the community to focus on the origin and meaning of the action to follow. Acolytes 1 and 2 (or other servers, if available) pick up ewer (jug) and basin and towels and accompany the celebrant to the place of the washing.

If the Washing is to take place at the end of pews (see above), the participants are asked to remove shoes etc.

If the washing is to take place at a separate location (e.g. Sanctuary), participants should be led with a minimum of fuss: they should be helped to feel dignified yet relaxed.

4. The celebrant begins the washing with the help of the Acolytes. The latter should help only so far as there is a need: overmuch activity can obscure the dignity of the basic action. Both servers stand well back until required: at the same time they

are alert to offer help to the celebrant and any participants who seek it.

5. The washing completed, the celebrant returns to the chair, washes his hands (servers assisting) and puts on the chasuble; or this can be carried out at the side, since the celebrant's hand-washing has no liturgical significance. Meanwhile, if the feet washing has taken place away from the pews, the participants are conducted back to their places.

6. The general intercessions (bidding prayers) are introduced by the celebrant. The Creed is not recited.

7. The Presentation of the Gifts may include, in addition to the bread and wine, special gifts for the poor, in this way celebrating the theme of service. The precise content of the gifts will depend upon the local community and might comprise the results of a particular Lenten project. If this form of the Presentation takes place, adequate, visible and dignified space should be provided for the gifts but not on the altar.

8. Note the special texts for use with Eucharistic Prayer I.

9. Mass continues in the usual way until the end of the Communion Rite. During Communion the thurifer prepares the thurible for the procession. After Communion, to make it easier for the

celebrant to carry the Blessed Sacrament in the procession, it is advisable to use only one ciborium, though this may be difficult to arrange.

10. The celebrant recites the Prayer after Communion; the Roman Missal/Sacramentary does not indicate where this should take place but under the circumstances the altar is preferable to the chair. The celebrant puts incense in the thurible, kneels before the altar and censes the Blessed Sacrament three times. A server places the humeral veil over the celebrant's shoulders.

11. Thurifer, cross-bearer, Acolytes and torch-bearers stand ready in processional order.

12. The celebrant picks up the ciborium and the procession to the chapel of repose begins. The order of procession is similar to that in no.1, on p.27, with the addition of torch-bearers flanking the celebrant (if there is room) and the omission of the Book of the Gospels.

13. At the chapel of repose the cross-bearer and Acolytes move to one side to allow access by the celebrant. The thurifer is positioned so as to assist at the following incensation. Individual churches will make their own arrangements for positioning other servers and clergy according to the dimensions of the chapel.

14. The celebrant places the ciborium on the altar or at the entrance to the tabernacle, leaving the door open, and a server takes the humeral veil from him. He puts incense in the thurible, kneels and censes the Blessed Sacrament. He pauses for a short period of silent prayer, after which he closes the tabernacle and all make a single genuflection (except bearers and Acolytes) and process to the sacristy.

15. The stripping of the altars no longer carries with it the ceremonial once customary. All crosses should be removed or covered so that the showing of the cross on Good Friday may be more clearly focussed.

16. Adoration before the Blessed Sacrament may take place through the night, though for reasons of safety or because of the lack of transport this is rarer nowadays. The Roman Missal/Sacramentary states that there should be no solemn adoration after midnight. This too is rare, informality often being preferred.

HOLY THURSDAY check list

SERVERS

- ❍ Acolyte 1
- ❍ Acolyte 2
- ❍ Cross-bearer
  (book-bearer)
- ❍ Thurifer
- ❍ 2 assistants for washing of feet
- ❍ Possible: 2 or 4 torch-bearers
- ❍ Possible: 2nd thurifer for procession

SACRISTY

- ❍ White chasuble
- ❍ Processional cross
- ❍ 2 Acolyte's candles
- ❍ Lighted thurible
  (2nd thurible prepared during Holy Communion)

SANCTUARY

- ❍ All as at normal Mass plus:-
  sufficient altar breads for Thursday and Friday (holy oils ready for presentation at beginning of Mass, see HOLY THURSDAY, Introduction on p.24) bread and wine for Presentation of Gifts (special gifts for the poor, see no.7 on p.29)

Holy Thursday check list continued

- ❍ Ewer and large basin for washing of feet
- ❍ Towel for each participant having feet washed
- ❍ Seating for participants
- ❍ Apron or amice for washing of feet
- ❍ Humeral veil

CHAPEL OF REPOSE

- ❍ Empty tabernacle
- ❍ Tabernacle key
- ❍ 2 lighted candles

GOOD FRIDAY

INTRODUCTION

SIMPLICITY IS THE KEY-NOTE to today's celebration, a simplicity that focuses one's attention upon the stark but deeply moving fact of the death of our Saviour on the cross. The official title, The Celebration of the Lord's Passion, says it all. Serving should therefore be marked by a certain reticence, and devoid of any hint of flamboyance. Once again it is worth reminding ourselves that the ministry of serving exists to promote and support the prayer and worship of the whole community: that is a particular challenge on Good Friday. If the servers, through their restrained ministry, draw attention away from themselves and lead it toward the texts and the meaning of the principal rites, they will have done their job well.

The celebration is divided into three parts: the Liturgy of the Word, the Veneration of the Cross, Holy Communion. To put it a slightly different way: we listen to an account of the passion and death of Jesus, respond in prayer, visually and actively acknowledge his cross as the means of our salvation, and are united with him in Holy Communion.

The Liturgy of the Word is conducted in this way in no other part of the Roman liturgy. Minus entry chants, greetings, and penitential rite of the regular Mass, it appears strange and unusual. Yet historically it is very likely that we have here the earliest form of the Liturgy of the Word still in use in the Roman rite: for a period of time, this was almost certainly the way in which every celebration of Mass began until the other elements were added over the passage of time. The Veneration of the Cross originated in Jerusalem where the reputed true cross was accorded special honour on this day. Holy Communion was a much later addition, and even today this part of the rite gives the appearance of an afterthought. Some communities omit Holy Communion from the Good Friday celebration.

The part of the Veneration of the Cross called the Showing is carried out in one of two ways.

In the first form, the celebrant stands at the front of the altar, the veiled cross is brought to him and he performs the unveiling and proclamation, standing in the same place.

In the second form, the celebrant goes to the door of the church where he takes up the unveiled cross and processes with it through the church, halting in three stages to sing the proclamation.

Choice of option depends upon local circumstances, but the second form is to be preferred because it has a greater visual impact and takes the action of the liturgy into the heart of the community.

THE LITURGY

1. Procession forms:

   ✻ *Acolyte 1 – Acolyte 2*
   (without candles)

   ✻ *Other servers*

   [Readers and Ministers of Communion]

   ✻ *Non-presiding clergy*

   ✻ *Celebrant*

   Nothing is carried, except the books for the opening prayer and the readings, if these are not already in place in the sanctuary.

2. On arrival in the sanctuary, all bow to the altar and go to their designated places. A book-bearer stands near the presidential seat, ready for the opening prayer.

3. All kneel when the presiding celebrant kneels or prostrates on the floor, the latter being the more impressive action. Substantial pause for prayer.
4. Rising, the celebrant goes to the presidential chair and says the opening prayer (book-bearer) with hands joined.
5. The readings take place as usual.
   The Passion is read as on Palm Sunday.
   A homily follows.
6. The General Intercessions are led by the celebrant at the chair (book-bearer) or the lectern. A deacon may read out the intentions; in which case the deacon does this from the lectern, or ambo, and the priest reads the prayers at the chair. The Roman Missal / Sacramentary adds the altar to the possible locations but it is difficult to justify this, except in churches with extremely restricted space.

   Although not mentioned in the Roman Missal/Sacramentary, it seems appropriate that where a deacon is not present a lay reader should announce each of the intentions. A different voice from that of the celebrant adds texture and avoids the dominance of a single voice.

   The Roman Missal/Sacramentary also says that the people may stand or kneel during the General Intercessions; because standing is more usual during the General Intercession (Bidding Prayers) at Mass, the same posture may be preferable on Good Friday.

7. **First form of veneration of the cross:** three servers, or two servers plus a deacon or an assisting priest, exit the sanctuary, bowing to the altar on the way, and go to the place where the veiled cross and lighted candles are waiting (sacristy or other suitable place). Carrying the veiled cross and candles, they immediately return to the sanctuary without any bow or genuflection. The cross is handed to the celebrant: the bearer returns to his/her place: the Acolytes stand either side of the celebrant, some few paces away and facing each other.
8. The celebrant unveils the cross in three movements: first the upper part, then the right arm, finally the entire cross. After each movement, he says or sings, 'This is the wood of the cross…' etc, the community responds, 'Come, let us worship', and, all except the celebrant, kneel in brief, silent prayer.
9. **Second form of veneration of the cross:** the celebrant (or deacon) and two servers go to the church door where they pick up the uncovered cross and two lighted candles. They process through the church to the sanctuary, pausing once near the church entrance, once in the middle, and once on arrival in the sanctuary, each time the celebrant (or deacon) singing/saying, 'This is the wood of the cross…' etc with the community response as in no.8, above.

10. In either form of veneration, the cross is then placed or held by servers at the most suitable place for individual veneration by the rest of the community. This place need not be at the entrance to the sanctuary, though that is often the most suitable. The two lighted candles are placed in a convenient position either side of the cross.

    Servers may hold the cross to facilitate the people's veneration (particularly for the very young and others with particular physical needs), and to wipe the cross after it is kissed, though one has doubts about the hygienic usefulness of this exercise. Alternatively, the cross may be left on its own, perhaps standing in a support.

    If servers support the cross for a large crowd of people, they should be substituted after a while; it can be very tiring, especially for younger servers.

    The form of individual veneration can vary – genuflection, bow, kiss: local custom and individual choice decide.

    The celebrant leads the individual veneration, followed by other clergy and then servers, not for reasons of hierarchical precedence, but to set the pattern for an orderly, processional approach to the cross.

11. Where very great numbers are involved and individual veneration by all is near impossible, a group of representatives of the community may venerate the cross (e.g. members of a parish

council). After the celebration the cross is left in a convenient location for all to venerate at their own convenience.

Only one cross may be used at the veneration. The use of several crosses to speed up the veneration seriously damages the liturgy.

12. **Holy Communion:** servers place on the altar its cloth, a corporal and the Roman Missal / Sacramentary.
    Servers, flanked by those bearing the two candles, bring the cross and place it on or near the altar. A larger cross, if placed on the altar, might be out of proportion to it and obscure the Holy Communion liturgy.

    The candles are likewise placed on or near the altar.

13. The deacon/priest/celebrant and two servers depart for the chapel of repose, genuflecting as they leave the sanctuary. On arriving at the chapel, they genuflect and one server assists the deacon/priest/celebrant to put on the humeral veil; he opens the tabernacle, takes out the ciborium, the servers pick up the lighted candles and all process back to the sanctuary.

    The ciborium is placed on the altar; a server retrieves the humeral veil; the candle-bearers place their candles on or near the altar.
    Red stoles distributed to any other clergy

14. The Holy Communion liturgy proceeds as in the Roman Missal/Sacramentary: viz. Lord's Prayer; Deliver us Lord...; Lord, Jesus Christ, with faith in your love and mercy...; This is the Lamb of God...; distribution of Communion.

    After Holy Communion, any Sacrament remaining is taken to a place of reservation apart from the church; any suitable minister may do this, accompanied by two servers with lighted candles. Only as a last resort may the ciborium be placed in the main tabernacle.

15. The celebrant leads a few moments of quiet reflection then says the prayer 'Almighty and eternal God...' followed by the Prayer over the People. There is no final blessing or dismissal.

16. Servers, other ministers and the celebrant form up in the sanctuary in processional order, genuflect together and exit in silence.

17. Later, the altar is stripped of candles and cloths. It is customary to the leave the cross on or near the altar, unless it is to be venerated after the celebration (cf. no.12, on p.40). However the liturgical books do not single out the cross when mentioning the stripping of the altar, so perhaps it too should be removed. This makes sense if devotionally we are to regard the period after the Celebration of the Lord's Passion as the time of burial, not crucifixion.

GOOD FRIDAY check list

SERVERS

- ❍ Acolyte 1}
  Cross
- ❍ Acolyte 2}

- ❍ Acolyte 1}
  Ciborium
- ❍ Acolyte 2}

- ❍ Book-bearer, altar preparers

SACRISTY

- ❍ Red vestments
- ❍ Roman Missal/Sacramentary (if carried by bearer)
- ❍ Lectionary and/or Book of Gospels (if carried by Deacon/reader)

SANCTUARY

- ❍ Altar totally bare of all crosses, candles, and cloths
- ❍ Altar cloth and corporal to one side of the sanctuary (credence table) in readiness for Holy Communion
- ❍ Water and towel for possible ablutions
- ❍ Red stoles for priests and/or deacons receiving Holy Communion

Good Friday check list continued

- ❍ Roman Missal/Sacramentary
  (if not carried by bearer)
- ❍ Lectionary and/or Book of Gospels
  (if not carried by Deacon/reader)

First form of Veneration

- ❍ Veiled cross (usually white, though no colour stipulated in Roman Missal/Sacramentary)
- ❍ 2 acolyte's candles (lighted)
  all in a convenient but discrete place
  (sacristy or other suitable place)

Second form of Veneration

- ❍ Unveiled cross
- ❍ 2 acolyte's candles (lighted) at or near the church door

Chapel of Repose

- ❍ Humeral veil (red or white)
- ❍ 2 acolyte's candles (lighted)
- ❍ Tabernacle key

Place of reservation apart from church

- ❍ Access
- ❍ Secure reservation
- ❍ No candles

The Easter Vigil

INTRODUCTION

THE CHURCH TEACHES that 'the liturgy is the summit toward which the activity of the Church is directed: it is also the fount from which all her power flows'[1]. And the summit of the liturgy is the Easter Vigil. Like all summits, there is the ascent – Lent and the related liturgies of Holy Week – and the descent – the on-going celebration of the resurrection, not only during the Easter season but throughout the rest of the Church's year. The Easter Vigil is the peak celebration of Christ's victory over sin and death.

Altar servers will have their interest and enthusiasm aroused if their leaders (priests as well as lay ministers) are convinced of the importance of this celebration. The uniqueness of the earlier parts of the celebration are certainly attractive to servers who are accustomed to the regular round of liturgies throughout the course of the year: the colourful, even exciting, contrast with the normal Sunday routine seizes their interest. This can be enhanced by a simple yet well-

1 Vatican II, Constitution on the Sacred Liturgy, 10.

focussed explanation of the liturgy before any practice takes place (and practice is surely necessary).

First, we remind ourselves that the celebration of the Easter Triduum (the Evening Mass of the Lord's Supper on Holy Thursday, the Celebration of the Lord's Passion on Good Friday and the Easter Vigil) constitutes a single celebration. All that has gone before during the previous two days is resolved and summed up in the glorious resurrection from the dead of the Lord Jesus Christ.

Second, very many parish communities will have been involved in the Rite of the Christian Initiation of Adults[2]; servers may well have witnessed the celebration of various stages of this journey of faith. Now they are to play a part in its outcome with the celebration of the sacraments of initiation through the initiates' first participation in the death and resurrection of Christ.

Third, and in tandem with the second point above, the season of Lent will have been one of renewal for the whole community, a time of prayer, self denial and alms-giving during which baptised Christians will have reflected on the dignity to which they have been called. The Easter Vigil is the moment when this

2 *Rite of Christian Initiation of Adults, approved for use in the dioceses of England and Wales, Scotland*, Geoffrey Chapman, London, 1987. Referred to hereinafter as RCIA.

reaches a climax with the baptism of new members and renewal of the baptismal promises by the rest of the community. We recapture (or are captured by) the joy of the resurrection, Christ's victory over sin and death.

The Vigil is in four parts: service of light, liturgy of the word, initiation, Eucharist. The two earlier parts are prayerful and meditative, providing a sort of platform for the more active parts of initiation and Eucharist.

Admittedly the service of light is filled with action, yet action which leads to personal reflection. Not much is said during the blessing of the fire, the lighting of the candle and the procession: fire and light do their own work on the hearts and minds of the participants.

This is a useful reminder that the best celebrations are those in which the liturgy is allowed to speak for itself. This is especially true of the Easter Triduum when fussy and intrusive serving obscures the full vision of the liturgy.

In planning the celebration consideration should be given to the generous use of the symbols. For example, as large a fire as possible; a real Easter candle; using the lighted candles as long as possible before giving way to electric light (or daylight, if the Vigil is timed to conclude at dawn); a more ample choice of readings; the generous use of water at the baptism and renewal of promises.

The same can be said of the procession of light: locating the fire at some distance from the church, if at all possible, enables a longer procession and more readily recalls to mind that the risen Christ is the pillar of fire leading God's chosen people to the promised land.

The location of the water for baptism may require thought and planning. If the font is in full view of the community, as is increasingly the case, all well and good. If it is not, a dignified container for the baptismal water should be placed in full view of the people.

Planning this celebration is challenging because large sections are special to this day, and although every liturgical celebration should be the fruit of cooperation between all ministries, the Easter Vigil will lose much of its impact if ministers have not previously consulted together and listened to one another's ideas. Good celebration grows out of unity and reinforces that unity.

A practice for the candidates for initiation and their godparents is essential. They need to know what is to happen, where they will be located, what they are to do, what they are to say.

The Liturgy

1. **Blessing of the Fire and Lighting of the Candle.** Prepare the fire, making sure it is well alight before the start of the liturgy. A lay person with no other liturgical responsibilities is best suited for this task
2. The location of the fire determines much of what takes place at the beginning of the Vigil. Some communities can make use of grounds, parkland, or the local school playground; other churches immediately open out onto a busy city street. It is not possible to give advice for each and every eventuality. Whatever the situation, effort should be made to involve the community in the action as far as possible. Early arrivals anxious to reserve a seat in the church and therefore reluctant to go outside for the blessing of fire and the lighting of the candle are to be persuaded to forgo their security of tenure, at least for a short time.
3. The assembling of celebrant, servers and other ministers also depends on the location of the fire, although the sacristy is the best place because there last minute instructions can be more conveniently given.
4. Church lights out.
5. Ensure each person (including servers with free hands) has a candle.

6. At the fire:

⁜ *Celebrant*

(deacon)

⁜ *Easter candle bearer*

⁜ *Thurifer with unlighted thurible*

⁜ *Book-bearer with Missal/Sacramentary*

⁜ *Electric torch bearer*

⁜ *Other clergy*

⁜ *Keeper of fire*

7. Celebrant leads the people in the sign of the cross and greets them as usual.

He introduces the Vigil.

Fire is blessed.

Celebrant inscribes the Easter candle with the cross, A (alpha) and Ω (omega), and numerals of the year.
(This may be omitted but is included by most communities.)

Easter candle is lit from the fire.

Charcoal is lit from the fire and placed in thurible.

Celebrant puts incense on charcoal.

8. Celebrant/deacon takes the Easter candle, raises it and sings 'Christ our light'.
The Missal / Sacramentary says this happens three times: at the beginning of the procession, at the church door, on arrival at the altar. However in longer processions a more frequent repetition with lengthy pauses after each repetition is very effective; even after arrival at the altar it may be useful to repeat it as long as is necessary for the entry of the people.

9. **Procession:**

❊ *Thurifer*

❊ *Easter candle carried by celebrant/deacon*

❊ *Other clergy*

❊ *Servers*
(no cross or acolytes' candles)

❊ *Community*

10. Candles of all participants (except candidates for initiation) are lit from the Easter candle on entering the church, signifying that as members of the Church we are enlightened by Christ. However this may be the least satisfactory part of the liturgy. A large crowd of people, squeezing through the church entrance and attempting to light their candles from the single Easter Candle not only causes a long delay but frequently

reduces the action to an untidy scrum.

One solution is for servers to light their own candles from the Easter candle, then stand in such a position that the incoming people are able to light their candles from the servers' (this needs to be well planned beforehand and the servers given clear instructions). It is not an ideal solution, but at least the lighted candles have their source of light in the Easter candle.

Delay as long as possible switching on electric lights: until the 'Glory to God in the highest', if possible.

11. The Easter candle is placed in its stand either near the lectern or in the centre of the sanctuary.

    Servers go to their places.

    Thurifer goes to the celebrant who puts incense in the thurible.

    Celebrant/deacon censes the Easter candle and the book for the Easter Proclamation (Exsultet).

    Celebrant/deacon/or another minister sings the Easter Proclamation (Exsultet). Note there is a long and short form, as well as variations when the singer is not a priest or deacon.

    An electric torch may be needed, but candles are to be preferred.

    The Missal/Sacramentary says that after the proclamation all may put out their candles, but see no.10, on p.50.

12. **Liturgy of the Word** follows the celebrant's introduction, with its regular pattern of reading, response, prayer.

13. After the final Old Testament reading, the celebrant intones 'Glory to God in the highest'.

    Bells are rung, if that is the custom locally.

    Altar candles are lit.

    Opening prayer.

    New Testament reading.

    Solemn Alleluia.

    Incense in thurible.

    Gospel with incense, but no acolyte's candles.

    Homily.

14. IMPORTANT NOTE: if there is to be initiation the RCIA book is used from this point until the renewal of baptismal promises by the entire community: the Missal/Sacramentary does not contain all the texts for the Liturgy of Baptism.

    A book-bearer is almost essential: no further reference will be made here.

15. **Liturgy of Initiation** *without reception of anyone into full communion of the Catholic Church.*

There are three ways of beginning this part of the rite (i. ii. iii., below): i. and ii. assume the font is at least a little way from the sanctuary, while iii. is for a sanctuary location.

i. Celebrant, servers and other ministers go directly to the font.
Deacon/or other minister calls candidates and godparents
(and parents if any candidates are children) to the font.
No text for this in the books.
All stand so as not to block the view for the community

Litany of the Saints. (RCIA p.124)

Invitation to prayer and water blessing (RCIA pp.124 and 126A).

Go to no.16 on page 55.

ii. Deacon/other minister calls candidates and godparents (and parents if any candidates are children) close to the sanctuary. No text for this in the books.

Procession forms:

❊ *Easter candle (deacon/other)*

❊ *Candidates and godparents (children's parents)*

❊ *Servers*

❊ *Book-bearer*

❊ *Celebrant*

Litany of Saints sung during the procession (RCIA p.124).
At font all stand so as not to block the view for the community.
Easter candle placed in temporary stand near the font.
Invitation to prayer and water blessing (RCIA pp.124 and 126A).
Go to no.16, on next page.

iii. Deacon/other minister calls candidates and godparents (and parents if any candidates are children) to the sanctuary. No text for this in the books.
All stand so as not to block the view for the community.
Invitation to prayer and Litany of Saints (RCIA p.124).
Water blessing (RCIA p.126A).

16. RCIA recommends that the celebrant dip the Easter candle in the water one or three times as he invokes the power of the Holy Spirit.

17. At the end of blessing A go straight to RCIA p.136, Renunciation of Sin. (Ignore the confusing 'Profession of Faith' at the foot of RCIA p.135).

    Blessing options B, C, D, E, are not for use at the Easter Vigil.

18. **Renunciation of Sin:** celebrant questions the candidates, choosing one of three formulas.

19. [Anointing with oil of catechumens (RCIA p.137). *Not always included: check with celebrant.*

    Assist celebrant with oil and provide cloth/cotton wool to dry oil from his hands.]

20. **Profession of Faith and Baptism** (RCIA p.137-139): ideally each candidate individually makes the profession of faith and is immediately baptised. Large numbers suggest a unison response, followed by individual baptisms.

    Ensure the celebrant has the name of each candidate, perhaps provided by the lead catechist.

    Baptism by total immersion, though sadly infrequent in UK, is the Church's preferred option. Details RCIA p.138-139.

Baptism by pouring: godparents place their right hand on the shoulder of their candidate as the celebrant baptises.

Towel ready for each newly baptised.

21. [*Anointing with chrism* (RCIA pp.139-140): only if Confirmation is to be celebrated at a later date. The integrity of the rite of initiation presumes that the sacrament of confirmation is bestowed immediately after baptism.]

22. **Clothing with baptismal garment** (RCIA p.140): local custom decides the manner and form of this. Sometimes omitted.

23. **Presentation of lighted candle** (RCIA p.141): celebrant holds or touches the Easter candle and invites godparents to light a candle from it and present it to their newly-baptised godchild.

    Newly-baptised remain in/before the sanctuary.

24. **Confirmation** is celebrated at the place of baptism (RCIA pp.142-143).

    Chrism brought to the celebrant.

    Ensure celebrant is provided with names of candidates for confirmation.

    At the moment of anointing the godparents place their right hand on the shoulder of their godchild.

Celebrant may need to wash his hands after the sacrament.

The newly initiated return to their places.

25. If either of the options 15 i. or ii. on p.53, is used, celebrant, servers, ministers now return to sanctuary in procession.

26. If the number of candidates for confirmation is large, assisting priests share the bestowal of the sacrament.

27. **Renewal of Baptismal Promises:** (RCIA p.251) or return to Missal/Sacramentary for this section.

People stand with lighted candles: servers with tapers lighted from Easter candle take light to community.

Celebrant leads the renewal.

Celebrant takes baptismal water (container and sprinkler provided by a server) and sprinkles the people.

He concludes with prayer (RCIA p.254 or Missal / Sacramentary).

28. If the baptismal water is blessed in the sanctuary and the font is in another part of the church, the water may now be taken 'reverently' (Missal/Sacramentary) by a deacon and/or servers to the font. Alternatively, it can be left in the sanctuary to be moved at a more convenient time.

29. The Creed is not said.
General Intercession (Bidding Prayers) follow.
Go to no.37, on p.60.

30. **Liturgy of Initiation and the Rite of Reception into full Communion of the Catholic Church.**

All as in nos.15 to 23 inclusive, on pp.53-56.
This takes place in the sanctuary.
Confirmation of the newly baptised is postponed until later in the liturgy.
The newly baptised retire temporarily to their seats.

31. **Renewal of Baptismal Promises,** as in no.27, on p.57 (RCIA pp.251–254).

32. **Act of Reception:** celebrant invites the candidates for reception, together with their sponsors, to the sanctuary (RCIA p.254).

He invites them (no text given) to make the special profession of faith, singly or as a group. (RCIA p.254).

Servers ready with copies of the text for candidates.

Celebrant [lays his hand on the candidate's head if they are not to be confirmed shortly and] pronounces the *Act of Reception* (RCIA p.255).

33. **Celebration of Confirmation:**

The newly baptised are invited (no text) back to the sanctuary.

He addresses them as in RCIA p.255.

Celebrant confirms the newly baptised and the newly received as in nos. 24–26, on pp.56–57 (RCIA p.255-257).

The liturgy continues as in no.28, on p.57.

34. **Easter Vigil without initiation or reception.**

There are two possibilities:

i. the font and water are blessed
ii. only the water is blessed

35. i. (font and water to be blessed) Special invitation to prayer in Missal/Sacramentary at beginning of section, Liturgy of Baptism.
Litany of Saints follows: note special invocations at its end.
General Intercessions.

36. ii. (water only to be blessed) Litany of Saints omitted.
Go straight to the Blessing of Water in Missal / Sacramentary.
Renewal of baptismal promises follows, as in no.27, on p.57.
General Intercessions.

37. Liturgy of the Eucharist

The newly initiated may take part in the procession of the gifts.

Note the special texts for Eucharistic Prayers I to IV in Missal/Sacramentary in the section Ritual Masses, Christian Initiation, Baptism (pp.756–757 Roman Missal, and pp.830–831 Sacramentary for USA); in the section for the Easter Vigil only Eucharistic Prayer I is mentioned.

Communion: ensure the newly-baptised and newly-received are guided in their first reception of the Eucharist.

Solemn dismissal.

EASTER VIGIL check list

SERVERS

- ❍ Easter candle-bearer (at fire and in procession to font) [see: no.15, on p.53]
- ❍ Thurifer
- ❍ Book-bearer
- ❍ Electric torch-bearer (in case firelight / candlelight are insufficient)
- ❍ Servers for various tasks, e.g. bearer of stylus, grains of incense [see: no.7, on p.49]
- ❍ Water-bearers [see: no.27, on p.57]
- ❍ Acolyte candles and processional cross are not used at the Easter Vigil.

SACRISTY

- ❍ White vestments

[Items for blessing of fire etc., if these are not already at fire:

- ❍ Easter candle
- ❍ Stylus
- ❍ Grains of incense
- ❍ Empty thurible
- ❍ Incense
- ❍ Tapers
- ❍ Candle for celebrant [candles for others including servers]

- ❍ Missal/Sacramentary

Continued ➢

Easter Vigil check list continued

AT FIRE

- ❍ Fire
- ❍ Charcoal
- ❍ Tongs for transferring lighted charcoal to thurible
- ❍ [Other items as SACRISTY, on previous page, if not carried out by servers]
- ❍ Fire extinguisher !

SANCTUARY

- ❍ All as for Mass (candles not alight)
- ❍ Missal/Sacramentary
- ❍ Lectionary
- ❍ RCIA book
- ❍ General intercessions (bidding prayers)
- ❍ [separately printed text for profession of faith (RCIA p.254) if there is to be reception into Church]
- ❍ EITHER: font prepared with water (if located in sanctuary)

  OR: suitable container for blessing of water in sanctuary
- ❍ Towel/s for newly baptised
- ❍ Easter candle stand near lectern, or centre of sanctuary

Easter Vigil check list continued

- ❍ Empty container for water sprinkling at renewal of promises
- ❍ Oil of catechumens (see: 19, on p.55)
- ❍ Chrism
- ❍ Cotton wool, or alternative, for celebrant's hands after administering oils

FONT

If apart from the sanctuary but used for blessing of water, baptism and confirmation (see: 15 i and ii, on p.53):

- ❍ RCIA book
- ❍ Water in font (or in container for pouring at blessing)
- ❍ Towel/s for newly baptised
- ❍ Easter candle stand (in addition to one in sanctuary)
- ❍ Empty container for water sprinkling at renewal of promises
- ❍ Oil of catechumens (see: 19, on p.55)
- ❍ Chrism
- ❍ Cotton wool, or alternative, for celebrant's hands after administering oils

Exsultet